# Macbook Pro
# User Guide

**Simplified Macbook Pro for Seniors &
Beginners: Master MacOS in 25 Minutes**

## Benjamin F. Trigger

# Macbook Pro

# User Guide

Simplified Macbook Pro for Seniors & Beginners:
Master MacOS in 25 Minutes

Benjamin F. Trigger

This book is dedicated to all Macbook users/owners

# Contents

# INTRODUCTION

Did you just buy a MacOS, Big congratulations. Whether what you have is a Macbook Air, Pro or Mini, this guide succinctly explains the steps involved in unlocking your device like a pro.

You'll learn about key MacBook Air features, such as the Touch ID, discover how to use macOS and its built-in apps, plus much more. By the time you've finished reading MacBook Air Guide, you'll be an expert in nearly everything MacBook and macOS related.

Enjoy your read.

# 1

# MACBOOK SETUP PROCESS

It's not the easiest thing to set up a MacBook.

And it can get harder if you are a newbie with the whole apple thing. You can just easily follow the instructions presented on the screen. But you may not understand what they mean.

In this guide, well talk about how you can set up you Mac. We'll be talking about each step you may encounter on the road

1. To turn on your Mac, press the **Power** button.

2. You will have to select a language. The language you choose here will be the language that will show on your computer. When you have selected your language, select **Continue**

3. The next thing is to set Keyboard Input. What this means is the command that will be sent to the monitor when you press a key on the keyboard. This can be set no matter how the physical keyboard is.

4. You then you want to choose a Wi-Fi network. If you use a Wi-Fi network, you just need to select your network then enter in the password. But if you make use of Ethernet. You will have to choose Other Network options. Then choose the option for **Ethernet**. If this process takes time and

says, Looking for Networks, just wait for it, it is normal.

5. If you are setting your mac as a new device, then choose **Don't Transfer Any Information on the Next Screen.** Choose **Continue**

6. Check the box for **Enable Location Services** on this mac. The reason why you would want to consider setting up this option is because, it will be used for Siri, suggestions, Maps and other things. But still if you don't feel comfortable with your location being tracked, you don't need to check the box

7. You will now be asked to sign in with your Apple ID. Enter it and select **Continue**

8. Agree to the terms and conditions. If you would like to see more about the document, select **More.**

9. Enter in a full name for your MacBook. But if you had already logged in with your Apple ID. This may not be necessary as if should filled.

10. Input an account name. This too should already filled if you are logged in with your Apple ID.

11. To secure your computer, you will be asked to input a password. This password is the administrator password that will help you create other accounts and get access to some options on your Mac.

12. If you would like to remember your password when you forget, you may want

to choose **Hint**. What this will do is remind you when you type in the wrong password. To help you to access your computer when you forget your password, you can also choose the option for **Allow Apple ID to reset this password**. But if someone else can access your Apple ID, this may be not as secure but it's worth a shot.

13. Check the box that reads **Set Time Zone Based On Location**. But if you would like this work, you would need to have enabled Location Services. When you eventually enable it, your current location will determine the date and time shown on your Mac. Hit **Continue**.

14. If you are signed in, iCloud should start syncing. It shouldn't take long, probably just a few minutes. You could also see

Setting up account. You just wait and let all be done

15. Check the box for **Turn on FileVault Disk Encryption** and **Allow my iCloud account to unlock my disk**. If you would like iCloud to unlock your disk, just know that it's no different than telling iCloud to reset your Mac password. Hit **Continue**

16. Check the box that reads **Store Files from Documents and Desktop in iCloud**. This will store all the contents in your documents folder and your desktop. This feature is part of the option made available by Optimized Storage.

17. And of course, you want to enable **Siri** on the MacBook. But if you're not a big fan, then you may just leave it disabled. Siri is

your own virtual assistant on your computer. Select **Continue**.

When you get to this stage, you should give yourself a pat on the back because you've scaled through the MacBook set up. The computer should try to set up the Mac and sync iCloud. There a chance that this process will not take 3 seconds so be patient.

# 2

# USING THE TRACKPAD & THE TOUCH

# Trackpad

The trackpad on your Mac has quite a number of gestures embedded in it. And the more you can fully optimize trackpad gestures, the more productive your usage of the Mac can be. So one of the best thing you can do is learn some of them.

**Quick rotating**

It's not new to have apps that that can be used for photo editing. The billion humans who use Photoshop still exist. And one thing that many struggle with is being able to rotate easily. There's a trick to use your trackpad for it. Just use your thumb and one finger and do the rotate motion.

**Zoom in**

Another thing you would like to do is zooming with the trackpad. I actually found out this trick by mistake but it's just the same you would do if you were zooming with your phone. Use your fingers to pinch and unpinch to denote zoom in and zoom out. You can also double tap very quickly to zoom in.

## Scrolling

If you're in a website or something like a text document, you can just make use of two fingers to swipe up and down. With this, no need to find the scroll bar at the right.

## Display the desktop

You can use your trackpad to expose the desktop and other open windows. You just need to swipe down with about 4 or 3 fingers. This will show up all the windows open. Use a thumb and 3 fingers to unpinch the trackpad

## Clicking

You can just tap the trackpad with 1 finger to denote the left clicking motion. You can also right click when you tap with 2 fingers.

# Touch bar

If your MacBook pro is the 13 inch and 15 inch kind, you should have the touch bar. This bar is that new touch-based bar that you find at the area where the function keys used to be. It's a great feature and you can start making use of it from the get go.

**The basic controls**

At the right of the touch bar, you find the control strip. With it, you can make changes to settings and also increase the brightness or volume. And you can also call up Siri with it. All you need to do is tap it to show the buttons.

You can also get additional options for the strip, but you should know that the additional options depends on the particular app you are using. You just need to press the arrow key to find those options

**Option for typing suggestions**

The typing suggestions option that shows on the touch bar is simply awesome. You can get suggested words as you type. It usually guesses the next word you will type and most times it's correct. If you would like to see those suggestions, hit the keyboard icon and the arrow. Tap the suggestions to enter them in the field

You may also need to turn it on by yourself if it doesn't work

1. Enter **View**
2. Choose **Customize Touch Bar**
3. Select **Show Typing Suggestions**

**Use functions keys**

Normally, you would be expecting the function keys at the top row of the keyboard. But now it's the touch bar. So it is only normal for the touch bar to compensate for taking the function spot. And compensate it did, you can still get the function keys with this bar. You just press the **Fn** on the keyboard and then press your function key. This will work if you have set Fn to show function keys

**Customize it**

With some apps, you get the option to change what is presented on the touch bar. Of course you will want to take advantage of this and edit the touch bar.

1. Select **View** when you are in an app
2. Choose the option for **Customize the Touch Bar**
3. You will then be able to rearrange buttons, add or remove buttons

# 3

# ESSENTIAL SETTINGS & CONFIGURATIONS

# Show up battery percentage

If you are using the Mac, chances are you also use the iPhone. Even if you don't use an iPhone, you will have the option to display the battery percentage on or near the battery. It's so much better than trying to guess by looking at the bar.

If you would like to enable battery percentage,

1. On the menu bar, select the battery icon
2. Select the option for **Show Percentage**
3. Choose **Energy Saver**
4. Tick the box for **Battery Status In Menu Bar**

# Edit the touch bar

The touch bar in the MacBook is one of the best improvements of for Mac devices. While some consider it entirely useless, others are overjoyed. If you are one of the latter group, then you will want to customize it

1. Enter the **System Preferences**
2. Choose **Keyboard**
3. Select the **Customize Touch Bar Button**
4. Next step is easy as you'll be dragging buttons from the screen straight down to the bottom of the screen. They'll do a jump flip to the touch bar.

# Add items to the dock

On your MacBook, you should have a handful of apps on your dock. The dock is the display of apps that's shown at the bottom of the screen. These apps may not be your favorite but you would like your best apps here.

Remove an app by
1. Clicking the app from the dock and dragging it to the desktop
2. When the option for **Remove** appears, select it

Add an app by,
1. Opening said app
2. It should show up in the dock, Right click the app from the dock.
3. Select **Option**
4. Choose **Keep In Dock**

# Move the dock

Of course, everyone gets the dock at the bottom of the screen. That's how it is for everyone and you should be fine with it. But if you have a bigger screen, you may want to arrange the dock at the side instead.

Crazy move but we are doing it

1. Choose **System Preferences**

2. Select **Dock**

3. Choose **Left** or **Right** for the **Position On Screen Option**

4. While you're at it, why not change the size of the dock. Or tick the box for **Automatically Hide and Show Dock** to the hide the dock when you don't need it.

# Turn on browser favicon

If you have no idea what favicons are, it's those little symbols shown at the tabs of browsers. It shows the logo of the site. Enabling this option is not a do or die matter but it will at least help you know which tabs are open and you'll be able to manage them.

But the thing is that safari does not display the favicons by default. If you don't mind, leave this and move on to the next. But if you want enable it,

1. Enter **Preferences**
2. Find the tab for **Tabs**
3. Tick the box for **Show Website Icons In Tabs**

# Enable Siri

You have Siri on your computer. If you enabled it during set up, you should be able to start using this assistant. But that's not the case with all of us. You may have skipped that step. Or maybe, you don't want to have Siri on your computer and on your iPhone at once.

1. Go to **System Preferences**
2. Choose **Siri**
3. Check the box for **Enable Ask Siri** or uncheck it if you are for disabling

If you are for Siri, you may be interested in being able to use it better. To help you do this, you should look into Siri Voice and Language and Keyboard.

# 4

# USEFUL TIPS & TRICKS FOR OPTIMIM EFFICIENCY

# Take screenshots

It's very easy to take screenshots these days. Everyone needs to take screenshots at some point so it's only reasonable for manufacturers to make it reachable. But while taking screenshots of the entire screen is pretty easy, trying to take a screen shot of just a specific area of the screen is quite a process.

If you wanted to take screenshots on operating systems like Windows, you'll take the screenshot then find the snipping tool to cut off an area of the image you don't need.

On the Mac however is a lot easier. You just need to press **Shift + Cmd +4**. If you would still like to get the shot of the entire screen, you can just use **Cmd +Shift + 3**

# Use those bizarre characters

On the keyboard of your Mac, you have the regular alphabets and numbers. You also get other symbols like the dollar sign, question mark and the likes. But that's all for when you're typing English words. There other words that we say everyday and we don't know the how to type it in.

Take for example cliché, not everybody knows how to get the mark atop the E.

1. You just go to the **Edit** menu an app.
2. Go to special characters
3. Use whatever character you need

# Edit file icons

You know the Mac is truly beautiful both inside and out. The design you get by default do a pretty good job. That's one of the reasons why some buy the laptop in the first place. But if you would like to use another icon for some files, here's how you do it

1.  Right click on a document
2.  Select **Get Info**
3.  Copy the preview image
4.  Select the current document thumbnail
5.  Press **Cmd + V** to paste the image in the the **Get Info**

# Calculate and convert

Odds are you already know that you can do the simplest calculation with Spotlight. This function was available for some time now but since the introduction of macOS High Sierra, things got better.

You can convert from one unit to another by typing in something like '19 stone to pounds'. There's another option that's really cool. As you type in the amount you would like to convert, the system will present some handy alternatives and suggestions.

So if you were typing in $107, you'll be given the amount in Pounds, Euros, and other currencies. If you want to convert to a specific currency, you just have to type in $107 to Euros

# Use Windows

Of course it's not the norm to run Windows on the Mac and no fan of Apple will have the desire to. But there'll be some software and favorite games that are only available on Windows without an option for Mac.

Two options you have here; leave it or install Windows. You can run use Bootcamp assistant to run Windows full or you can use a Virtualizataion app like Virtual Box or VMware fusion.

# Sign on PDFs

It's funny how, although in technology, we still need to squiggle on a paper to get things set on stone. But if you ever need to sign a PDF, you don't need to start connecting to a printer and printing. You can just sign it directly form Mail

1. You just drag the PDF to the email
2. Hover on top of and a button should appear. Click this
3. You'll then get other options; one of them is to sign documents.
4. Another great thing is the option to hold a different signed piece of paper to the Mac's webcam and it will cut it out the background.

# Rename files in a batch

Previously, renaming files in a group will have you installing a third party app. it's either that or you use AppleScript to roll your script. But now, you can just highlight files in a batch then right click and choose Rename.

When you select Rename, you can replace any text that was there, add a new text or use some kind of format

# Easy share with friends and family

With the macOS and OS X, you get the option to share files with friends. With the share button, you can share to your contacts. If you don't know what the share button is, it's takes the shape of an arrow moving up and leaving the box.

Also the Mac will track the people you share stuff with and also how you share it. This is great as you can now easily share with friends you contact regularly. If you are one who sends links and other contacts to friends, you can find this option at the bottom of the share window so that you can pick it up easily.

# Be armed with split screen

With recent changes, it's very easy to use spit screen to view side by side two apps or windows. When you press and hold the left click motion on the green maximize button for an app at the upper left corner, you will be able to drag it and set to the area you want it to display.

You can then pick up the second app to show up on the other side. One bonus that the split screen feature gives you apart from the fact that you can work with 2 apps at once, is the fact at the menu bar and the launcher is obscured. Which is a good thing as you can get more free area for the screen.

# PDF annotations

The ability to preview is just great and with the Mac os Mojave. You can preview images, PDFs, and you can also view annotations for PDFs. That is if the PDF is agreeable with Acrobat the PDF app from Adobe.

You just need to ensure that you can see the **Edit** toolbar in the View menu. You will then notice that you have the option to draw arrows, thought bubbles, shapes and others. If you are the color kind, you can also use the option to choose different colors.

# Get the password for devices

There's one thing that makes the Mac to stand out. It is the ability for it to recall your passwords with the Keychain feature. With this feature all of your private details will be stored. That's cool but the reason why it's much cooler is when it comes to the matter of Wi-Fi connections

If you would like to recall your Wi-Fi password or you are in an unfamiliar area, you can use this Keychain to find out your passwords

1. Fire up the **Keychain Access**. You can find the Keychain Access by searching for it with spotlight
2. Look for the name f the connection
3. Click the **iCloud Keychain** twice according to the SSID you want.
4. Choose **Show Password**. Enter the password for Keychain and you'll be able to see the Wi-Fi password.

# Set keyboard shortcut easily

With keyboard shortcuts, everyone knows how much time they can save. But you can do more than the shortcuts set by the developers. If there's this menu you use regularly, you can just set a shortcut for it.

1. Enter the **System Preferences**
2. Choose **Keyboard**
3. Select **Application Shortcuts**
4. Use the **+** button to include a shortcut
5. From the dropdown list, you can select the app that it will be applied to.
6. Then you select a key combination to trigger the command.
7. Select **Add**

# Change the grouping settings for Notification center

Previously, notifications are grouped by app in the notification center. But that's some time ago and now, Apple has switched things up a bit. Instead of grouping by app, it groups by date. So all the notifications you get today will show up first so that you can see what you missed

But if you want a different sort order

1. Enter the **System Preferences** area
2. Choose **Notifications**
3. Edit the sort order to fit your desire. Find the menu for **Notification Center Sort Order**.

# Receive and send SMS on your Mac.

If you're sent a message to your iPhone, you find it in the green bubble and not the blue area. This is the case if you are sent an iMessage. Previously, SMS will only show up on the iPhone and you then have to reply.

But in recent times, you can get it sent to you Mac and to other iOS devices. But you want to have your iPhone set to iOS 8.1 or higher. When you are signed into your account of iMessage,

1. Go to **Settings**
2. Choose **Messages** on you iPhone
3. Turn it on.

# Tweak the file type of the screenshot

The thing with screenshots on the macOS is that it is saved as PNG. This is the default file type and those who weren't so pleased, had to cope with it. But you can change it to suit your needs.

1. Move to **Terminal**
2. You'll want to type in 'defaults write com.Apple.screencapture type JPG' and select enter.
3. When you're done with that, you can just restart your Mac.
4. When your Mac is restarted, the change will take effect

# Give conversations names

It's only normal to have hundreds of iMessage conversations happening at the same time. But sometimes you may find it hard to track the person that said a particular thing, where he said it and even when he said it. This proves to be the case when you use multi- people chats.

But now, you can give group chats names. You just need to select the details at the upper right area. Then type out the name you want.

You can also apply this for individual or seasonal conversations and rename it to something like Meeting for the Baseball Final on 29.

# Volume change in smaller increments

The volume keys on the keyboard of the Mac are a cool option. They provide a really handy way to adjust the volume. But the thing with this is that the difference between a volume increase can be quite big. One quick tip to help with this is to press down Option + Shift.

If you don't want the get the audible feedback that everyone gets when they adjust the volume, you can turn it by going to the System Preferences. But you can turn it off and on temporary when you press Shift as you change the volume.

# Family sharing on the macOS

With the family sharing feature available on the macOS, about 6 people can share purchases. If you are parent, you would come to love this feature as it gives you the power to reject an app store purchase that the kids could make with your own card.

It's also great as you can use the family calendar and find out where everybody is. If you would like to set it up,

1. Enter the **System Preferences**
2. Move on the **iCloud Area**
3. Choose **Set Up Family**
4. Go through with the prompts to complete setup.

# Change the output from the menu

If you own a set of headphones or speaker and you set it up with your Mac, something you would find yourself doing regularly now is switching between multiple outputs and inputs. This is also the case if you have a microphone or headset connected.

You just have to press and hold Option and select the volume adjuster from the menu bar. This will bring it to the audio list of outputs and inputs.

# Store just about anything in the iCloud drive

With the new macOS, you can save any file you want into the Documents or Desktop folder. When you save the files, they can be automatically synced. It's great to able to create your own folders and save things through the Documents and Desktop folders.

These files will also be synced to the rest of the Macs linked with the same Apple ID. You can also access it when you go through iCloud.com

# Disclaimer

This book is not an overall guide to all Macbook tricks and troubleshooting

## About The Author

Benjamin Trigger been writing tech related books for some 15 years now. Some of his research materials have appeared in international magazines and blogs.